■

Stone Circles of England

A Journey Through Time, Mystery, and Legacy

BY MILA ORION

■

MY INTENTION:
ETERNAL BLESSINGS TO YOU ALWAYS,
DEAR READER.

Copyright © 2023

Table of Contents

Dedication

To those who wander among ancient stones, seeking whispers of the past,
To the scholars and enthusiasts who dedicate their lives to unraveling the mysteries of our ancestors,
And to my family and friends, whose unwavering support has made this journey possible.

May this book inspire curiosity, reverence, and a deeper connection to the timeless legacy of human creativity and spirituality.

Introduction

Stone Circles, those enigmatic arrangements of standing stones, have captured human imagination for centuries. Scattered across the landscapes of England, these ancient monuments are a testament to the ingenuity, spirituality, and social organization of the prehistoric communities that built them. This book aims to explore the fascinating world of Stone Circles in England, delving into their history, purpose, and the mystery that continues to surround them.

Overview of Stone Circles in England

England is home to some of the most famous and well-preserved Stone Circles in the world. From the iconic Stonehenge to the lesser-known circles hidden in the rural landscapes, these structures provide a window into the past, allowing us to glimpse the beliefs, rituals, and daily lives of our ancestors.

Historical Context and Importance

The Stone Circles of England date back to various periods, primarily the Late Neolithic and Early Bronze Age, around 3000 to 1500 BCE. They were constructed during a time of significant social and technological change, reflecting a complex understanding of astronomy, geometry, and community gathering.

The importance of these circles extends beyond mere historical curiosity. They are symbols of cultural heritage, connecting us to a time when humanity's relationship with the land, the cosmos, and each other was expressed through these monumental works.

Purpose and Meaning of Stone Circles

The exact purpose of Stone Circles remains a subject of debate and fascination. Were they astronomical observatories, ceremonial sites, or perhaps communal gathering places? Theories abound, and this book will explore various interpretations, drawing on archaeological evidence, historical records, and contemporary research.

Methodology of Research

This comprehensive guide to the Stone Circles of England is the result of extensive research, collaboration with experts, and on-site exploration. It includes detailed descriptions of every known Stone Circle in England, along with their addresses, historical context, and vivid imagery.

The chapters that follow are organized by region and significance, allowing readers to embark on a journey through time and space, discovering the unique characteristics of each circle, and understanding their place within the broader European megalithic tradition.

Whether you are an archaeologist, historian, tourist, or simply someone intrigued by the ancient world, this book offers a captivating exploration of England's Stone Circles. Join us as we unravel the mysteries, appreciate the artistry, and celebrate the enduring legacy of these remarkable structures.

Chapter 1: The Great Stone Circles

The Stone Circles of England are not just historical artifacts; they are living monuments that continue to inspire awe and wonder. Among these, some stand out for their sheer size, complexity, and historical significance. This chapter explores the great Stone Circles of England, including Stonehenge, Avebury, and The Rollright Stones.

Stonehenge

Location: Salisbury Plain, Wiltshire, England

Description: Perhaps the most famous Stone Circle in the world, Stonehenge consists of a ring of standing stones, each around 13 feet high, seven feet wide, and weighing around 25 tons. The structure is aligned with the sunrise on the summer solstice, leading many to believe it may have been used as an astronomical observatory.

History: Built in several stages from around 3000 BCE to 1600 BCE, Stonehenge's purpose and construction methods remain subjects of intense research and debate. Recent discoveries suggest it may have been a place of healing or a symbol of unity among different tribes.

Address: Stonehenge, Salisbury, SP4 7DE, England

Avebury

Location: Avebury, Wiltshire, England

Description: Less famous but no less impressive, Avebury is the largest Stone Circle in Britain. It consists of a large henge containing three stone circles. The outer circle has a diameter of 1,082 feet, enclosing two smaller inner circles.

History: Dating back to around 2600 BCE, Avebury's purpose is still not entirely understood. Some believe it was used for rituals or ceremonies, while others think it may have had astronomical significance.

Address: Avebury, Marlborough, SN8 1RF, England

The Rollright Stones

Location: Near Chipping Norton, Oxfordshire, England

Description: The Rollright Stones are a complex of three Neolithic and Bronze Age megalithic monuments. The site includes the King's Men stone circle, the King Stone, and the Whispering Knights.

History: The stones are steeped in folklore and legend, with stories linking them to witches and kings. Archaeological studies suggest that the site was used for various purposes over the centuries, including ceremonial gatherings.

Address: Rollright Stones, Little Rollright, Chipping Norton, OX7 5QB, England

The great Stone Circles of England are more than mere stones; they are a testament to the ingenuity, spirituality, and social organization of the prehistoric communities that built them. Each site offers a unique glimpse into the past, and their mysteries continue to captivate researchers and visitors alike.

These monumental structures are not just historical landmarks but living connections to our shared heritage. They invite us to ponder the beliefs, rituals, and daily lives of our ancestors, and they challenge us to unravel the secrets they still hold.

Whether you visit them in person or explore them through the pages of this book, the great Stone Circles of England are sure to inspire awe, curiosity, and a deeper appreciation for the rich tapestry of human history.

Chapter 2: Stone Circles of Cornwall

Cornwall, with its rugged coastline and rich Celtic heritage, is home to some of England's most intriguing Stone Circles. These ancient monuments, set against the dramatic Cornish landscape, provide a fascinating insight into the region's prehistoric past.

Boscawen-Un

Location: Near St Buryan, Cornwall, England

Description: Boscawen-Un is a striking Stone Circle consisting of 19 stones, with a leaning central stone. The circle is known for its unique arrangement, with one of the stones being made of quartz.

History: Dating back to the Bronze Age, Boscawen-Un is believed to have been a significant site for rituals and ceremonies. Its alignment with certain astronomical events adds to the mystery of its original purpose.

Address: Boscawen-Un, St Buryan, Penzance, TR19 6EH, England

The Merry Maidens

Location: Near St Buryan, Cornwall, England

Description: Also known as Dawn's Men, The Merry Maidens is a perfect circle of 19 granite stones. Local legend tells that the stones are maidens turned to stone for dancing on the Sabbath.

History: Archaeological evidence suggests that The Merry Maidens dates back to the Late Neolithic or Early Bronze Age. It may have been used for ceremonial gatherings or as an astronomical calendar.

Address: The Merry Maidens, St Buryan, Penzance, TR19 6BQ, England

Trippet Stones

Location: Near Bodmin Moor, Cornwall, England

Description: The Trippet Stones consist of 11 standing stones arranged in a circle. The site is named after the old English word for dancing, reflecting the local folklore associated with the stones.

History: Thought to date back to around 2500 BCE, the Trippet Stones' original purpose remains unclear. Some believe it may have been used for rituals, while others see it as an astronomical site.

Address: Trippet Stones, Bodmin Moor, Bodmin, PL30 4HW, England

Cornwall's Stone Circles are not only remarkable for their historical significance but also for their connection to local folklore and legend. Each site offers a unique perspective on the beliefs and practices of the ancient communities that once inhabited this beautiful region.

The Stone Circles of Cornwall invite us to explore a world where myth and history intertwine, where ancient stones tell tales of dancing maidens, celestial alignments, and sacred rituals. They stand as enduring symbols of Cornwall's rich cultural heritage, beckoning us to delve deeper into the mysteries of our shared past.

Whether you are a seasoned explorer of ancient sites or new to the wonders of megalithic structures, the Stone Circles of Cornwall offer a captivating journey through time, space, and imagination.

Chapter 3: Stone Circles of Cumbria

Cumbria, a region known for its breathtaking landscapes and rich archaeological heritage, is home to some of England's most well-preserved Stone Circles. These ancient monuments, set against the backdrop of the Lake District's stunning scenery, offer a glimpse into the prehistoric communities that once thrived in this area.

Castlerigg

Location: Near Keswick, Cumbria, England

Description: Castlerigg Stone Circle is one of the most visually stunning megalithic sites in England. Comprising 38 stones in a slightly oval shape, it offers panoramic views of the surrounding fells.

History: Dating back to around 3000 BCE, Castlerigg is one of the earliest British circles. Its purpose is still debated, but it may have been used for ceremonies or as a meeting place for prehistoric communities.

Address: Castlerigg, Keswick, CA12 4RN, England

Swinside

Location: Near Millom, Cumbria, England

Description: Also known as Sunkenkirk, Swinside Stone Circle consists of 55 stones arranged in a near-perfect circle. It is one of the best-preserved monuments of its kind in England.

History: Built around 3200 BCE, Swinside's original purpose remains enigmatic. Some theories suggest it was used for rituals, while others believe it had astronomical significance.

Address: Swinside, Millom, LA19 5YJ, England

Long Meg and Her Daughters

Location: Near Penrith, Cumbria, England

Description: This intriguing site consists of a large standing stone known as Long Meg, surrounded by 69 stones arranged in an oval shape. Long Meg is adorned with mysterious symbols, adding to the site's allure.

History: Dating back to around 1500 BCE, Long Meg and Her Daughters is steeped in folklore. It is believed to have been a site for Druid ceremonies, though its exact purpose is still debated.

Address: Long Meg and Her Daughters, Penrith, CA10 1QX, England

Cumbria's Stone Circles are remarkable not only for their historical and archaeological significance but also for their connection to the natural landscape. Each site offers a unique perspective on the beliefs, rituals, and social organization of the ancient communities that once inhabited this region.

The Stone Circles of Cumbria are a testament to human creativity, spirituality, and connection to the land. They invite us to explore a world where ancient stones resonate with timeless wisdom, where history and nature intertwine, and where the mysteries of our shared past continue to inspire wonder and curiosity.

Whether you are drawn to the beauty of Castlerigg, the perfection of Swinside, or the legends of Long Meg and Her Daughters, the Stone Circles of Cumbria offer a captivating and enriching experience that transcends time.

Chapter 4: Stone Circles of Devon

Devon, with its rolling hills, moorlands, and rich archaeological heritage, is home to several intriguing Stone Circles. These ancient monuments, nestled within the beautiful landscapes of the region, provide valuable insights into the prehistoric communities that once inhabited this part of England.

Grey Wethers

Location: Near Postbridge, Dartmoor, Devon, England

Description: Grey Wethers consists of two distinct but closely spaced Stone Circles. Each circle contains 24 stones, and they are nearly identical in size and appearance, creating a unique and symmetrical visual effect.

History: Dating back to the Bronze Age, Grey Wethers' purpose is not entirely understood. Some believe the site may have been used for rituals, while others see it as a significant meeting place.

Address: Grey Wethers, Postbridge, Dartmoor, PL20 6SP, England

Scorhill

Location: Near Gidleigh, Dartmoor, Devon, England

Description: Scorhill Stone Circle is one of Dartmoor's most intact circles. It consists of 23 standing stones, some reaching up to 8 feet in height, arranged in an elliptical shape.

History: Built around 2000 BCE, Scorhill's original function remains a subject of debate. Its alignment with certain celestial events suggests it may have had astronomical significance.

Address: Scorhill, Gidleigh, Dartmoor, TQ13 8JN, England

Spinsters' Rock

Location: Near Drewsteignton, Devon, England

Description: Spinsters' Rock is a Neolithic dolmen rather than a Stone Circle, but its significance in the region warrants mention. It consists of three large supporting stones topped by a massive capstone.

History: Dating back to around 3500 BCE, Spinsters' Rock is one of the oldest megalithic structures in Devon. Local legend tells of three spinsters who erected the stones before breakfast, giving the site its name.

Address: Spinsters' Rock, Drewsteignton, Exeter, EX6 6PB, England

Devon's Stone Circles and megalithic structures are not only remarkable for their historical significance but also for their connection to local folklore and legend. Each site offers a unique perspective on the beliefs and practices of the ancient communities that once thrived in this picturesque region.

The Stone Circles of Devon invite us to explore a world where ancient stones stand as silent witnesses to rituals, celestial alignments, and the daily lives of our ancestors. They are enduring symbols of Devon's rich cultural heritage, beckoning us to delve deeper into the mysteries of our shared past.

Whether you are drawn to the symmetry of Grey Wethers, the grandeur of Scorhill, or the legends of Spinsters' Rock, the megalithic sites of Devon offer a captivating journey through time, space, and human creativity.

Chapter 5: Stone Circles of Derbyshire

Derbyshire, known for its scenic landscapes and rich industrial history, is also home to several significant Stone Circles. These ancient monuments, set within the beautiful Peak District, provide a fascinating glimpse into the prehistoric era of this part of England.

Nine Ladies

Location: Stanton Moor, Derbyshire, England

Description: Nine Ladies is a small but captivating Stone Circle consisting of nine standing stones, each around 3 feet high. The site also includes a nearby standing stone known as the King Stone.

History: Dating back to the Bronze Age, Nine Ladies is believed to have been a site for rituals and ceremonies. Local legend tells that the stones are nine ladies turned to stone for dancing on the Sabbath, a common theme in Stone Circle folklore.

Address: Nine Ladies, Stanton Moor, Bakewell, DE4 2LS, England

Arbor Low

Location: Near Bakewell, Derbyshire, England

Description: Arbor Low is one of the most important prehistoric sites in Derbyshire. It consists of around 50 white limestone stones, most of which are now lying flat. The site includes a henge and a central cove, adding to its complexity and intrigue.

History: Built around 2500 BCE, Arbor Low's original purpose is still debated. Some believe it was used for ceremonial gatherings, while others see it as an astronomical site.

Address: Arbor Low, Bakewell, DE45 1JS, England

Derbyshire's Stone Circles are remarkable not only for their historical and archaeological significance but also for their connection to the natural landscape. Each site offers a unique perspective on the beliefs, rituals, and social organization of the ancient communities that once inhabited this region.

The Stone Circles of Derbyshire are a testament to human ingenuity, spirituality, and connection to the land. They invite us to explore a world where ancient stones resonate with timeless wisdom, where history and nature intertwine, and where the mysteries of our shared past continue to inspire wonder and curiosity.

Whether you are drawn to the legends of Nine Ladies or the grandeur of Arbor Low, the Stone Circles of Derbyshire offer a captivating and enriching experience that transcends time. Their silent stones beckon us to delve deeper into the mysteries of our ancestors and to appreciate the enduring legacy of these remarkable structures.

Chapter 6: Stone Circles of Yorkshire

Yorkshire, a region known for its diverse landscapes and rich cultural heritage, is also home to several intriguing Stone Circles. These ancient monuments, scattered across the moors and dales of Yorkshire, provide valuable insights into the prehistoric communities that once thrived in this part of England.

The Twelve Apostles

Location: Ilkley Moor, West Yorkshire, England

Description: The Twelve Apostles is a prominent Stone Circle located on Ilkley Moor. Despite its name, the circle originally consisted of around 20 stones, of which only a few remain standing today.

History: Dating back to the Bronze Age, The Twelve Apostles' original purpose is not entirely understood. Some believe the site may have been used for rituals or as an astronomical calendar.

Address: The Twelve Apostles, Ilkley Moor, Ilkley, LS29 9RF, England

Druid's Altar

Location: Bingley Moor, West Yorkshire, England

Description: Also known as the Bingley Stone Circle, Druid's Altar consists of several standing stones arranged in a circle. The site offers stunning views of the surrounding landscape and is steeped in local folklore.

History: The exact age and original function of Druid's Altar remain subjects of debate. Some theories suggest it was used for ceremonial gatherings, while others believe it had astronomical significance.

Address: Druid's Altar, Bingley Moor, Bingley, BD16 3AA, England

Yorkshire's Stone Circles are not only remarkable for their historical significance but also for their connection to local folklore and legend. Each site offers a unique perspective on the beliefs and practices of the ancient communities that once inhabited this picturesque region.

The Stone Circles of Yorkshire invite us to explore a world where ancient stones stand as silent witnesses to rituals, celestial alignments, and the daily lives of our ancestors. They are enduring symbols of Yorkshire's rich cultural heritage, beckoning us to delve deeper into the mysteries of our shared past.

Whether you are drawn to the enigmatic Twelve Apostles or the legendary Druid's Altar, the Stone Circles of Yorkshire offer a captivating journey through time, space, and human creativity. Their silent stones beckon us to ponder the mysteries of our ancestors and to appreciate the enduring legacy of these remarkable structures.

Chapter 7: Lesser-Known Stone Circles

While England's most famous Stone Circles often capture the spotlight, there are many lesser-known circles that are equally intriguing and historically significant. These hidden gems, scattered across various regions, offer unique insights into the prehistoric era and deserve exploration and recognition.

Mitchell's Fold

Location: Near Chirbury, Shropshire, England

Description: Mitchell's Fold is a Bronze Age circle consisting of 15 stones, though originally there may have been as many as 30. Local legends and folklore add to the site's mystique.

Address: Mitchell's Fold, Chirbury, SY15 6DE, England

The Hurlers

Location: Near Minions, Cornwall, England

Description: The Hurlers is a complex of three Stone Circles situated on Bodmin Moor. The site's name comes from a legend that the stones are men turned to stone for playing a game of hurling on a Sunday.

Address: The Hurlers, Minions, Liskeard, PL14 5LE, England

Birkrigg Stone Circle

Location: Near Ulverston, Cumbria, England

Description: Birkrigg Stone Circle, also known as the Druid's Temple, consists of two concentric circles. The site offers panoramic views of Morecambe Bay and the Lake District fells.

Address: Birkrigg Stone Circle, Ulverston, LA12 9QZ, England

Duddo Five Stones

Location: Near Duddo, Northumberland, England

Description: This small Stone Circle consists of five large stones, standing in a picturesque landscape. The stones are heavily weathered, giving them a unique and ancient appearance.

Address: Duddo Five Stones, Duddo, TD15 2NR, England

Merry Maidens of Boscawen

Location: Near St. Buryan, Cornwall, England

Description: Not to be confused with the Merry Maidens near Penzance, this small circle consists of 11 standing stones and is located near the famous Boscawen-Un circle.

Address: Merry Maidens of Boscawen, St. Buryan, TR19 6BN, England

These lesser-known Stone Circles, though often overshadowed by their more famous counterparts, are rich in history, legend, and cultural significance. Each site offers a unique perspective on the beliefs, rituals, and social organization of the ancient communities that once inhabited various regions of England.

The hidden Stone Circles of England invite us to explore a world where ancient stones resonate with timeless wisdom, where history and nature intertwine, and where the mysteries of our shared past continue to inspire wonder and curiosity.

Whether you are a seasoned explorer of ancient sites or new to the wonders of megalithic structures, these lesser-known Stone Circles offer a captivating journey through time, space, and human creativity. Their silent stones beckon us to delve deeper into the mysteries of our ancestors and to appreciate the enduring legacy of these remarkable structures.

Chapter 8: The Archaeology of Stone Circles

The Stone Circles of England are not merely historical landmarks; they are intricate puzzles waiting to be solved. Archaeology plays a crucial role in unraveling the mysteries of these ancient structures, shedding light on their construction, purpose, and the people who built them. This chapter delves into the archaeological exploration of England's Stone Circles, highlighting key discoveries, tools, techniques, and interpretations.

Excavations and Discoveries

- **Stonehenge Excavations:** Unearthing artifacts, human remains, and evidence of earlier wooden structures.

- **Avebury's Hidden Secrets:** Discovering smaller stone and wooden circles within the larger complex.

- **The Rollright Ritual Site:** Evidence of continuous use and modification over millennia.

Tools and Techniques

- **Aerial Photography:** Using aerial views to identify hidden features and alignments.

- **Ground-Penetrating Radar:** Revealing buried stones and features without excavation.

- **Radiocarbon Dating:** Determining the age of organic materials found at the sites.

- **Landscape Archaeology:** Understanding the relationship between the circles and their surrounding landscapes.

Interpretations and Theories

- **Astronomical Observatories:** Analyzing alignments with celestial events like solstices and equinoxes.

- **Ceremonial and Ritual Sites:** Evidence of feasting, burial, and other ceremonial activities.

- **Social and Political Centers:** Theories about the role of Stone Circles in uniting communities or marking territories.

- **Healing and Pilgrimage Sites:** Some circles, like Stonehenge, are associated with healing practices and may have attracted pilgrims.

Challenges and Controversies

- **Preservation vs. Exploration:** Balancing the need for archaeological investigation with the preservation of these delicate sites.

- **Conflicting Interpretations:** Ongoing debates about the true purpose and meaning of Stone Circles.

- **Access and Ownership:** Navigating the rights and interests of landowners, governments, and indigenous groups.

The archaeology of Stone Circles is a dynamic and evolving field, offering tantalizing glimpses into the distant past. Each excavation, analysis, and interpretation adds a new layer of understanding, bringing us closer to the minds and hearts of the people who erected these enigmatic structures.

The Stone Circles of England continue to challenge and inspire archaeologists, historians, and enthusiasts alike. They stand as silent witnesses to human ingenuity, spirituality, and the timeless quest for knowledge and connection.

Whether you are an academic, a curious traveler, or someone drawn to the mysteries of the ancient world, the archaeological exploration of England's Stone Circles offers a rich and rewarding journey through time, science, and human creativity.

Chapter 9: Modern Interactions and Preservation

The Stone Circles of England are not relics confined to the past; they continue to resonate with modern society in various ways. From tourism and accessibility to conservation efforts and contemporary interpretations, this chapter explores how these ancient monuments interact with the present and the ongoing efforts to preserve them for future generations.

Tourism and Accessibility

- **Iconic Destinations:** Sites like Stonehenge attracting visitors from around the world.

- **Guided Tours:** Educating the public about the history and significance of Stone Circles.

- **Accessibility Challenges:** Balancing visitor access with the preservation of delicate sites.

Conservation Efforts

- **Legal Protections:** Designating Stone Circles as Scheduled Monuments or World Heritage Sites.

- **Restoration Projects:** Repairing and stabilizing stones to prevent further deterioration.

- **Community Involvement:** Engaging local communities in preservation and stewardship.

Modern Interpretations and Uses

- **Spiritual Practices:** Some circles continue to be used for spiritual and religious ceremonies, particularly by modern Druid groups.

- **Artistic Inspiration:** Stone Circles as subjects in literature, visual arts, and music.

- **Educational Resources:** Utilizing Stone Circles to teach history, archaeology, and cultural heritage.

Ethical Considerations

- **Cultural Sensitivity:** Recognizing and respecting the spiritual significance of Stone Circles to various groups.

- **Sustainable Tourism:** Managing visitor impact to ensure the long-term preservation of sites.

- **Archaeological Ethics:** Conducting research and restoration with integrity and respect for the sites and their histories.

The Stone Circles of England are living monuments, bridging the gap between the ancient and modern worlds. They continue to inspire awe, curiosity, and reflection, drawing people from all walks of life to explore their mysteries and appreciate their beauty.

The preservation and responsible interaction with these sites are not merely matters of historical interest; they are essential to maintaining a tangible connection to our shared heritage. The Stone Circles stand as enduring symbols of human creativity, spirituality, and the timeless quest for understanding.

Whether you visit these sites in person or explore them through the pages of this book, the modern interactions with and preservation of England's Stone Circles offer a rich and rewarding experience. They invite us to honor the past, engage with the present, and contribute to a legacy that will continue to inspire future generations.

Chapter 10: Stone Circles in the Broader Context

While England is home to some of the most famous and well-preserved Stone Circles, these enigmatic structures are part of a broader tradition that spans the British Isles and extends into continental Europe. This chapter explores the connections, similarities, and differences between Stone Circles in various regions, offering a comprehensive view of this fascinating aspect of prehistoric culture.

Stone Circles in Scotland

- **Callanish Stones:** Located on the Isle of Lewis, this complex includes multiple Stone Circles and rows.

- **Ring of Brodgar:** Part of the Heart of Neolithic Orkney World Heritage Site, this circle is one of the finest in Scotland.

Stone Circles in Wales

- **Bryn Cader Faner:** Known for its unique crown-like appearance, this Bronze Age circle is one of Wales' most iconic.

- **The Harold Stones:** A small alignment of three large standing stones, reflecting the diversity of megalithic structures in Wales.

Stone Circles in Ireland

- **Newgrange:** Though primarily known as a passage tomb, Newgrange is part of a complex that includes several Stone Circles.

- **The Grange Stone Circle:** Ireland's largest Stone Circle, located near Limerick, offers insights into the country's rich megalithic tradition.

Stone Circles in Continental Europe

- **Carnac Stones (France):** This extensive complex includes alignments, dolmens, and Stone Circles, representing one of Europe's most significant megalithic sites.

- **Goloring (Germany):** A rare example of a Stone Circle in Germany, providing evidence of the broader European context of these structures.

Comparative Analysis

- **Architectural Styles:** Examining the diversity in size, shape, and construction techniques across regions.

- **Cultural Connections:** Exploring shared themes, such as astronomical alignments and ritual uses, that hint at broader cultural connections.

- **Regional Variations:** Understanding how geography, local traditions, and available materials influenced the design and purpose of Stone Circles.

Conclusion: A Pan-European Legacy

The Stone Circles of England are part of a rich tapestry that weaves across the landscapes of the British Isles and Europe. They reflect a shared human endeavor to understand the cosmos, celebrate community, and connect with the spiritual world.

These ancient monuments, though separated by time and distance, speak to universal themes that continue to resonate with us today. They invite us to explore a world where stones tell stories, where history and legend intertwine, and where the mysteries of our shared past continue to captivate and inspire.

Whether you are drawn to the grandeur of Stonehenge, the complexity of Callanish, or the elegance of the Carnac Stones, the Stone Circles of Europe offer a captivating journey through time, space, and human creativity. They stand as enduring symbols of our collective heritage, beckoning us to delve deeper into the mysteries of our ancestors and to appreciate the enduring legacy of these remarkable structures.

Conclusion

Summary of Findings

The exploration of England's Stone Circles has taken us on a remarkable journey through time, space, and human ingenuity. From the iconic grandeur of Stonehenge to the lesser-known circles hidden across the landscape, we have uncovered a rich tapestry of history, archaeology, folklore, and modern interactions. These ancient monuments have revealed themselves to be far more than mere stones; they are living connections to our shared heritage, resonating with timeless wisdom and universal themes.

The Continuing Mystery and Allure of Stone Circles

Despite the extensive research and exploration detailed in this book, the Stone Circles of England continue to hold an air of mystery and allure. Their precise purposes, the meanings behind their alignments, and the rituals that may have taken place within them remain subjects of fascination and debate. This enigmatic quality is perhaps what draws us to them, inviting us to ponder the beliefs, aspirations, and daily lives of our distant ancestors. The Stone Circles stand as silent witnesses to a past that is at once foreign and intimately connected to our own human experience.

Future Research Directions

The study of Stone Circles is far from complete. New archaeological techniques, interdisciplinary approaches, and cultural perspectives continue to open fresh avenues for exploration. Future research may focus on:

- **Detailed Analysis of Lesser-Known Circles:** Many smaller and lesser-known circles await thorough investigation.

- **Digital Reconstruction and Virtual Reality:** Utilizing technology to recreate and explore Stone Circles as they may have appeared in their prime.

- **Community Engagement and Education:** Encouraging public involvement in preservation and appreciation of these sites.

- **Comparative Studies with Other Megalithic Structures:** Expanding our understanding by comparing Stone Circles with other ancient monuments worldwide.

Final Reflection

The Stone Circles of England are more than historical landmarks; they are gateways to understanding ourselves and our place in the cosmos. They challenge us to unravel their secrets, inspire us with their beauty and complexity, and remind us of the enduring human desire to connect with something greater.

As we close this exploration, we are left with a sense of wonder and a deeper appreciation for the rich tapestry of human history. The Stone Circles beckon us to continue our quest for knowledge, to honor the past, and to embrace the mysteries that still await discovery.

Whether you visit these sites in person or explore them through the pages of this book, may the Stone Circles of England continue to captivate your imagination, enrich your understanding, and connect you to the timeless legacy of human creativity and spirituality.

Appendice 1: Glossary of Terms

- **Alignment:** The arrangement of stones in a line or pattern, often related to astronomical events such as solstices or equinoxes.

- **Archaeoastronomy:** The study of how ancient cultures understood and utilized celestial phenomena, often applied to Stone Circles.

- **Barrow:** A type of burial mound often found near Stone Circles.

- **Bronze Age:** A period in ancient history (approximately 2300-800 BCE in Britain) characterized by the use of bronze tools and the construction of many Stone Circles.

- **Cairn:** A human-made pile or stack of stones, often used as a burial marker.

- **Cove:** A small, tightly arranged set of standing stones, often found within a larger Stone Circle.

- **Dolmen:** A type of megalithic tomb with a large flat stone laid on upright ones.

- **Henge:** A circular earthwork, often surrounding a Stone Circle, consisting of a ditch and bank.

- **Ley Lines:** Hypothetical alignments of geographical and historical sites, including Stone Circles, believed by some to have spiritual significance.

- **Megalith:** A large stone used in various prehistoric structures, including Stone Circles.

- **Menhir:** A single upright standing stone.

- **Neolithic:** The final part of the Stone Age (approximately 4000-2300 BCE in Britain), marked by the development of agriculture and the construction of megalithic monuments.

- **Passage Tomb:** A type of burial tomb consisting of a narrow passage made of large stones and one or multiple burial chambers.

- **Radiocarbon Dating:** A method used to determine the age of an object containing organic material by measuring the amount of carbon-14 it contains.

- **Scheduled Monument:** A legally protected archaeological site or historic building in the United Kingdom.

- **Standing Stone:** Also known as a menhir, a large upright stone, often part of a larger arrangement like a Stone Circle.

- **Stone Circle:** A prehistoric monument characterized by a circular or elliptical arrangement of standing stones.

Appendice 2: Index

A

- Arbor Low, see Derbyshire Stone Circles

- Archaeoastronomy, see Glossary of Terms

- Avebury, see Wiltshire Stone Circles

B

- Birkrigg Stone Circle, see Lesser-Known Stone Circles

- Boscawen-Un, see Cornwall Stone Circles

- Bronze Age, see Glossary of Terms

C

- Callanish Stones, see Stone Circles in Scotland

- Carnac Stones, see Stone Circles in Continental Europe

- Conservation Efforts, see Modern Interactions and Preservation

D

- Derbyshire Stone Circles

- Dolmen, see Glossary of Terms

- Druid's Altar, see Yorkshire Stone Circles

E

- Excavations and Discoveries, see Archaeology of Stone Circles

G

Printed in Great Britain
by Amazon